Fearless faith

Jonathan Stephen

Copyright © 2015 by Jonathan Stephen

First published in Great Britain in 2015 (Reprinted Once)

British Library Cataloguing in Publication Data

A record for this book is available from the British Library

ISBN: 9781910587317

Designed by Steve Devane

Printed in the UK by CPI Group (UK) Ltd, Croydon, CR0 4YY

10Publishing, a division of 10ofthose.com

Unit C, Tomlinson Road, Leyland, PR25 2DY, England

Email: info@10ofthose.com

Website: www.10ofthose.com

Fearless faith

Jonathan Stephen

CONTENTS

When Jesus saw the crowd around him, he gave orders to cross to the other side of the lake ...

Then he got into the boat and his disciples followed him.

Suddenly a furious storm came up on the lake, so that the waves swept over the boat. But Jesus was sleeping. The disciples went and woke him, saying, 'Lord, save us! We're going to drown!'

He replied, 'You of little faith, why are you so afraid?' Then he got up and rebuked the winds and the waves, and it was completely calm.

The men were amazed and asked, 'What kind of man is this? Even the winds and the waves obey him!'

MATTHEW 8:18, 23–27

The battle we all face

1

According to the New Testament, there are three great motivators in the Christian life – faith, hope and love. For instance, the Apostle Paul begins his first letter to the young church plant in Thessalonica by saying, 'We remember before our God and Father your work produced by faith, your labour prompted by love, and your endurance inspired by hope in our Lord Jesus Christ' (1 Thes. 1:3).

What we ultimately trust in, where our hope really lies and what we love most of all not only reveal our true selves but also determine the direction of our lives. I remember as a boy being highly impressed by the picture of a ship worker totally dwarfed by the massive marine propellers of an enormous ocean liner about to be launched. Though quite unseen when the vessel was afloat, these beautifully sculptured steel creations would be the means of its propulsion. In the same way, think of faith,[1] hope[2] and love[3] as the three huge propellers that drive the church of Jesus (and you as a member of that church) safely through the perilous seas of life. This is why we must take care to nurture and strengthen these greatest of all spiritual gifts. We need to make the best use we can of what are commonly called 'the means of grace' – such as biblical preaching that is applied to our lives, and genuine prayer. However, we must also remember that we are in a spiritual battle, and all of us get wounded and weakened at times. For this reason, Paul says it's vital that we don't let Satan 'outwit us' and that we simply can't afford to be naively 'unaware of his schemes' (2 Cor. 2:11).

we are in a spiritual battle, and all of us get wounded and weakened at times

Knowing he must target our cardinal graces of faith, hope and love if he is to cripple our Christian lives, Satan deploys a weapon that has always proved to be immensely effective against all three – FEAR!

The truth is that fear cannot coexist peacefully alongside faith, hope or love. There is a constant battle between them until one or other takes control. Countless Bible passages reflect this reality. For example, Psalm 42:11 reflects the conflict between fear and hope: 'Why, my soul, are you downcast? Why so disturbed within me? Put your hope in God, for I will yet praise him, my Saviour and my God.'

And in 1 John 4:18 the battle between fear and love is depicted: 'There is no fear in love. But perfect love drives out fear, because fear has to do with punishment. The one who fears is not made perfect in love.

In this little book, though, we are going to concentrate upon the conflict as it rages between fear and faith, perhaps the commonest battle of all in the lives of most believers. We're going to see how the battle can be won – and how, in fact, we might emerge from the spiritual paralysis that fear brings and instead enjoy the spiritual progress that comes from fearless faith. To help us do this, we are going to look at one of the best-known and most dramatic incidents in the Gospels: the stilling of a terrible storm upon the Sea of Galilee. And what *this whole event was orchestrated by Christ entirely as a faith-training exercise for his future apostles*

we need to realise from the start is that this whole event was orchestrated by Christ entirely as a faith-training exercise for his future apostles.

In days to come, Jesus' disciples would require exceptional bravery as they proclaimed the gospel of salvation to an unbelieving and often hostile world. They needed to learn how natural fear could be dispelled. Thus the essential question Christ puts to them on this famous occasion is, 'You of little faith, why are you so afraid?' (Mt. 8:26).

As we have already seen, the antidote to great fear is a strong faith in the true Person of Christ. That's something we all need to understand as we are buffeted, and often frightened, by the storms and challenges of life. But how can we develop such a fearless faith? Well, let's prepare to join the disciples on this sensational training exercise and find out! In doing so, we shall be guided throughout by a vital biblical principle.

Hebrews 12 urges us to 'run with perseverance the race marked out for us, fixing our eyes on Jesus, the pioneer and perfecter of faith' (vv. 1–2). In other words, in order to grow our faith, we shall be fixing our eyes exclusively on Jesus as we explore this amazing event.

Jesus plans our journey through life

2

Jesus' day had been massively busy with teaching and healing; the adoring and needy crowds were constantly pressing upon him (see Mt. 8:5–17). It's understandable that Jesus wanted to get away with his disciples for some rest. So, as evening approached, 'he gave orders to cross to the other side of the lake' (Mt. 8:18). This is the first thing we need to notice: Jesus was responsible for the travel arrangements!

It was his decision, his timing. What we also need to grasp, though, is that Jesus' decision was not based on his needs alone. Have you ever wondered whether he realised that a terrible storm was brewing or whether it took him by surprise? As the strategic training purpose of what follows begins to unfold, we are surely led to conclude

Faith is like a spiritual muscle – it needs exercise

that Jesus knew exactly what lay ahead. Though he could have easily postponed the trip until the following day, he deliberately decided to sail off with his disciples into probably the worst weather conditions that even the former fishermen among them had ever experienced. Why did he choose to do this? It may not sound terribly caring, but it was all part of the disciples' training! Faith is like a spiritual muscle – it needs exercise if it is to become strong and not waste away. If our lives were always pleasant and never challenging, our faith would scarcely be required and never grow. We would not be much use to the Lord in this life, nor would we be prepared for the life to come.

The Apostle Peter, who was in the boat that day, certainly learnt this lesson well. Many years later, he would write, 'Dear friends, do not be afraid at the fiery ordeal that has come on you to test you, as though something strange were happening to you. But rejoice inasmuch as you participate in the sufferings of Christ, so that you may be overjoyed when his glory is revealed' (1 Pet. 4:12–13).

A Christian's trials and troubles are a normal and necessary part of our training for glory. So let's be thankful that our times are in the Lord's hands, and not in our own (Ps. 31:15). What an easy ride we would give ourselves if they were, and how unprepared we would be for eternity. It is deeply reassuring to know that Jesus plans the itinerary of our lives. Facing each day in that knowledge will strengthen our faith for whatever it may hold. And whatever it may hold will strengthen our faith even more.

Jesus commands a successful outcome

3

Do you think anyone or anything could ever prevent Christ's intentions from being fulfilled? I ask the question because, on this particular occasion, Jesus didn't say to the disciples, 'Let's set off and see how far we can get!' No, 'he gave orders *to cross to the other side* of the lake' (Mt. 8:18, my italics). And yet, when it came to it, the disciples' faith was greatly lacking. Far from simply taking Jesus at his word and believing they would land safely, when the storm began they were instead convinced that his plans were about to be overturned.

The Apostle Paul once declared that he was 'confident of this: that he who began a good work in you will carry it on to completion' (Phil. 1:6). God is not like us in this respect. Even the most single-minded people have to sometimes admit that they simply don't have the resources to fulfil their dreams. But that is never God's problem. He has all the resources in the universe. After all, he created them and they are his. So whatever he intends to happen, most surely will.Therefore, once Jesus had ordered that he and the disciples should cross to the other side of the lake, there was no possibility of them sinking somewhere in the middle of it! The failure of the disciples to take Jesus at his word betrayed the fact that their view of him was still far too limited and earthbound. They had yet to realise that nothing could ultimately frustrate their leader's plans. Their faith had to be tested and strengthened by experience before they could even begin to grasp something of Jesus' unassailable authority. Just as the disciples were, in fact, certain to finish their journey safely, so are we. It may feel, at the moment, that the odds stacked against us are just too great. Even though somehow or other, by God's grace, we have so far managed to survive every difficulty, our present circumstances seem bound to overwhelm us.

But this is not the case!

Nor is it only God's personal love for his children that ensures their ultimate safety. It is also a question of God's honour. His very word is at stake. Can it be trusted or not?

As Jesus himself put it, 'I give them eternal life, and they shall never perish; no one will snatch them out of my hand. My Father, who has given them to me, is greater than all; no one can snatch them out of my Father's hand' (Jn. 10:28–29).

'no one will snatch them out of my hand'

In the same letter quoted in the last chapter, Peter wrote that 'through faith' all true Christians 'are shielded by God's power until the coming of the salvation that is ready to be revealed in the last time' (1 Pet. 1:5). Notice that it is *through faith*! Sometimes our faith is so weak that we can scarcely believe it. But reflect on the number of times the Lord has brought you through tremendous crises. You are still on the route that a sovereign, saving God has mapped out for you. So don't be afraid! Let your experience of God's goodness in the past feed your faith in his loving purposes for you now. While there is no promise that we shall be delivered *from* all our trials and troubles, by faith we shall pass safely *through* them. The Lord has given orders that we shall cross to the other side of whatever difficulty or danger threatens to engulf us. What more should we need than this promise? Our only problem is fear – our only solution is faith.

Jesus rides the storms with us

4

John Newton, the author of 'Amazing Grace', led an extraordinarily eventful life. For many years he was involved in the slave trade, yet eventually he became one of its most ardent opponents. But it was during a terrific storm off the coast of Donegal, which was threatening to destroy the ship he was on, that Newton first cried out to God for mercy. As Newton wrote, 'That 10th of March is a day much to be remembered by me; and I have never allowed it to pass unnoticed since the year 1748. For on that day the Lord came from on high and delivered me out of deep waters.'

It is little wonder, then, that this account of a similarly fearful storm on the Sea of Galilee spoke powerfully to him. In fact, so much was this the case that he based 'Begone, Unbelief', another of his famous hymns, upon it. It is worth reading every verse, but it begins:

Begone, unbelief!

My Saviour is near,

And for my relief

Will surely appear:

By prayer let me wrestle,

And he will perform;

With Christ in the vessel,

I smile at the storm.

In noticing one of the main features of the story, the fact that Jesus was with his disciples in the boat, the hymn writer highlights one of the most significant and commonly mentioned antidotes to fear in the Bible – the presence of the Lord. For instance, this instantly recalls the words of Psalm 23: 'Even though I walk through the darkest valley, I will fear no evil, *for you are with me*' (v. 4, my italics).

Knowing the storm was brewing, we read that Jesus 'got into the boat and his disciples followed him' (Mt. 8:23). Mark too recounts this incident.

According to his version of events, when the tempest was at its height, the disciples asked: 'Teacher, don't you care if we drown?' (4:38). This was a pretty foolish question when Jesus was, literally, in the same boat!

Though we cannot see him, Jesus is just as surely with us! The promise to God's people has always been: 'Never will I leave you; never will I forsake you' (Heb. 13:5). Then who could forget Jesus' final words in Matthew's Gospel: 'And surely I am with you always, to the very end of the age' (28:20)? To put it crudely, therefore, if we go down, Jesus goes down with us! And I think you will agree with me that this could never happen... Are you a disciple of Jesus? He is with you in your deepest trouble. He is not about to step out of the boat. What could be more reassuring than that? It's time to say 'begone' to fear and unbelief! With Christ in the vessel, believe me, you may smile at the storm.

Though we cannot see him, Jesus is just as surely with us!

Jesus shares our humanity

5

I imagine that most of us would be wary of buying an expensive product from a doorstep salesman. And surely none of us would think of handing over our house or car keys to a total stranger! It is obviously unwise to trust people we hardly know, no matter how plausible they may sound. So, if Jesus is merely a passing acquaintance of yours, it would be quite unreasonable to expect you to have a strong and practical faith in him. Such a faith should not, and cannot, be built on vague and temporary religious hopes or feelings. No, the only firm foundation for strong faith is a clear and certain knowledge of Jesus and who he is. It was only because the Apostle Paul could say, 'I *know* whom I have believed' that he was able to go on and make one of the greatest faith claims in the whole of Scripture: 'I *know* whom I have believed, and am convinced that he is able to guard what I have entrusted to him until that day' (2 Tim. 1:12, my italics). By this Paul meant he had given himself body and soul to Jesus because, based entirely on his personal knowledge of him, he was certain that Christ would preserve him both in this life and the life to come.

Ultimately, nothing strengthens the believer's faith more than a full realisation and understanding of the Saviour's unique identity. Perhaps that is why no other miracle reveals the twin natures of Christ,

> *Ultimately, nothing strengthens the believer's faith more than a full realisation and understanding of the Saviour's unique identity*

his meekness and majesty, more starkly than this one in the storm. We shall marvel at his divine power in chapter 7 but, at this point, as Jesus sleeps from sheer exhaustion after such a long and tiring day, we are simply meant to observe his utter humanness – and to reflect on what that means for us.

That the Son of God was prepared to lay aside

his glory and become a human being is, in itself, an unmistakable indication of his astonishing love for us. But, more specifically, he became a man because only a perfect man could bear in our place the terrible penalty our sin deserved. And, in the process, he willingly shared in all the infirmities, and endured all the trials and temptations that sinful human beings have brought upon themselves.

Had the disciples, in the boat in the midst of the storm, known these truths about Jesus, do you think they would have panicked as they did? Would they not rather have rested humbly in his love for them, and in the certain knowledge that his saving purposes could not possibly be frustrated? The story is told of a passenger who was convinced one stormy night that the ship he was on was going to sink. His alarm was immediately allayed, however, when a crew member informed him that the captain was fast asleep in his cabin. If the captain was asleep, he reasoned, clearly there could be no real danger.

A sleeping Jesus presented an opportunity for the disciples to exercise faith. They failed to do so because, at that stage in their lives, their knowledge about him was insufficient. Perhaps they had some excuse, but we do not. Are you full of fear when you should be full of faith? Then get to know more about Jesus. If you particularly want to know more about Christ's humanity, and how this knowledge can strengthen your faith on a daily basis, then reading Hebrews 2 would be a good place to start:

> Since the children have flesh and blood, he too shared in their humanity so that by his death he might break the power of him who holds the power of death – that is, the devil – and free those who all their lives were held in slavery by their fear of death (Heb. 2:14–15).

This passage tells us that faith in a Saviour who is fully human enables us to overcome what is probably the most basic of human fears – the fear of death. (In fact, the whole of Hebrews 2 should be studied closely, because it explains why every aspect of our salvation depends on Jesus' human nature.)

Jesus addresses our lack of faith

6

If you look closely at verse 26 in Matthew 8, you may discover something you have never noticed or thought about before. To tell you the truth, I had missed it completely myself, even though I must have read the passage scores of times over the years.

Without thinking about it, I had always imagined that having been rudely awakened from his deep sleep, the first thing Jesus did was to leap up and sort out the violent storm raging around them. But that isn't what Matthew records. He specifically states that it is only *after* Jesus has addressed his disciples – 'You of little faith, why are you so afraid?' – that he famously stills the storm – '*Then* he got up and rebuked the winds and the waves, and it was completely calm' (my italics). Note that as the parallel accounts of Mark and Luke have no indicators of timing at this point, they in no way contradict Matthew. The celebrated nineteenth-century preacher, C.H. Spurgeon, explained it like this: 'He spoke to the men first because they were the more difficult problem to deal with!' We might smile at that but it is surely true. When have the blind forces of nature ever failed to obey the will of their Creator? Yet, ever since the Fall, it has been instinctive for human beings to do exactly that. Of course we are the greater problem to God! Our natural tendency is to rebel and to imagine we can live without any reference to him. That is the very essence of our sin, which first severed our connection from the only Source of life and love, and then triggered the dreadful and infinitely costly rescue plan we call the gospel. Of course the winds and the waves would obey Jesus – but would this lowly group of fishermen?

Let's try to analyse what they were thinking,

to assess the state of their hearts. Had they possessed absolutely no faith in Jesus at all, they would scarcely have bothered to wake him in the first place. If, as experienced sailors upon those treacherous waters, they were at the end of their tether, what would be the point of seeking the advice and assistance of a mere carpenter's son?

On the other hand, as we have already seen, had their faith been strong they would also have let him sleep on. In other words, the way they went to Jesus, roused him and complained to him, shows us that they had a faith that was genuine but far too small. It was a true faith but one that was nevertheless much too weak and ineffective to overcome the fear which filled their hearts and paralysed them – a faith that fully merited Jesus' rebuke, 'You of little faith, why are you so afraid?' Don't get me wrong, a little faith in Jesus is a lot better than none! A weak and timid faith placed in Jesus because it has grasped something of who he is and what he achieved on the cross is a very precious thing. It means the difference between salvation and judgement, between heaven and hell.

The problem arises, however, when a believer

is content to remain in such a state. I have often heard Christians of many years' standing almost boasting of the weakness of their faith. Some will say, 'Oh, I am just a simple believer; don't bother me with complex doctrine and difficult questions.' Others will protest that it's not the strength of faith that matters but where it is placed – and make that a lifelong excuse not to grow their faith. Still others appear not to have realised that there is such a thing as a scale of faith from weak to strong, and are therefore totally ignorant of its implications, as I will explain. To those who would say a simple, undeveloped faith in Jesus is enough, we must ask, 'Enough for what?' Is it enough for personal salvation? Perhaps. But is it enough for a God-honouring, joyful, fulfilling, fruitful and fear-free Christian life? That I very much doubt. And what kind of Christian is it who is simply satisfied with securing their own passage to glory without showing any serious concern for the spiritual destiny of those around them?

A careful reading of Matthew's Gospel will show that the author deliberately highlights Jesus' efforts to grow the faith of his disciples. Matthew shows that this lay at the very heart of the three-year training course in New Testament church planting that he himself had undertaken. For example, though the original name-calling is somewhat softened in our English translations, in Matthew's Gospel Jesus repeatedly addresses his disciples as 'little faiths' (6:30; 8:26; 14:31; 16:8; 17:20). He is not insulting them but is simply frustrated that they seem to be taking so long to possess and exercise the strong faith they are eventually going to require. Remember that Jesus was preparing his disciples to change the world, and for that their faith needed to be strong! The same is true for us if we are ever to have the courage and expectation to attempt great things for the Lord.

> *Jesus was preparing his disciples to change the world, and for that their faith needed to be strong!*

But didn't Jesus say that faith 'as small as a mustard seed' (Mt. 17:20) was enough? To understand Jesus' exact meaning here, let's look at the miracle where, following the disciples' inability to do so, Jesus heals a demon-possessed boy. (You may want to pause to read it in Matthew 17:14–20, along with the parallel account in Mark 9:14–29.)

The story is all about faith: no faith, new faith, little faith and 'mustard seed' faith. First, Jesus laments that the whole generation of Jews he lived among was 'unbelieving and perverse' (Mt. 17:17). Then, when the unfortunate boy's father says to Jesus, 'if you can do anything, take pity on us and help us' (Mk. 9:22), Jesus is astonished and infuriated. '"If you can"?' says Jesus. 'Everything is possible for him who believes' (Mk. 9:23). At this point the man famously exclaims, 'I do believe; help me overcome my unbelief!' (Mk. 9:24), and Jesus heals his son.

When the disciples later ask him why they couldn't drive out the demon, Jesus typically tells them it is because of their 'little faith' (Mt. 17:20).

Jesus typically tells them it is because of their 'little faith' (Mt. 17:20)

And, he adds, what they need instead is 'faith like a mustard seed'. Jesus had used this same image earlier when describing the explosive power of the kingdom of heaven (Mt. 13:31–32). Like the mustard seed, the kingdom of heaven starts small but grows exponentially.

Similarly, what the disciples needed was not their totally inadequate 'little faith' but 'faith like a mustard seed', which would grow until it could accomplish the seemingly impossible. (When some translations, including the NIV, add the interpretation '*as small as* a mustard seed' in Matthew 17:20, my italics, they render its meaning impenetrable. Jesus is self-evidently not saying that his disciples needed to replace their 'little' faith with a faith that was 'small' ...)

If 'little faith' were enough to overcome the fear that paralyses our Christian life and service, then Jesus would not have constantly told the apostles in no uncertain terms that it was not. Nor would they have asked him on at least one occasion to *increase* their faith. (See if you can guess Jesus' answer to that request before looking it up in Luke 17:5–6!)

So let us not be content with the crippling results of a fearful, little faith. The living faith we first received when Christ saved us was, like a seed, designed to grow and bear fruit. Though God alone gives the growth, we are called to nurture and exercise this precious gift. That way he is glorified and we are blessed:

For this very reason, make every effort to add to your faith goodness; and to goodness, knowledge; and to knowledge, self-control; and to self-control, perseverance; and to perseverance, godliness; and to godliness, mutual affection; and to mutual affection, love. For if you possess these qualities in increasing measure, they will keep you from being ineffective and unproductive in your knowledge of our Lord Jesus Christ (2 Pet. 1:5–8).

Jesus is sovereign over all

7

The account of the calming of the storm now reaches its dramatic climax. We saw in chapter 5 how Jesus displayed his full humanity as he slept in the stern of the storm-tossed boat, exhausted by the demands of an extraordinary day of teaching and healing. Now, at last, he unmistakably declares his full identity.

Perhaps no other miracle so clearly reveals Jesus as the God who created and sustains the universe. According to Mark's record of the event, 'He got up, rebuked the wind and said to the waves, "Quiet! Be still!" Then the wind died down and it was completely calm' (4:39). Here was no mere coincidence, no fortunate timing. As has often been pointed out, though a fierce wind may drop suddenly, a disturbed body of water takes far longer to return to a placid state. But on this occasion all motion seemed to cease immediately, both in the air and in the sea, as Jesus uttered just a couple of simple words. We do not even read that he had to raise his voice... But while this undoubted miracle is mightily impressive in its own right, it is the mind-blowing significance which underlies it that we really need to grasp.

Consider this: with the words of his mouth Jesus created order and harmony out of the chaos of the waters – just as he had 'In the beginning' (Gen. 1:1–2; Jn. 1:1–3; Heb. 1:1–2, 10).

In other words, the miraculous stilling of the storm is a mini replay of the part played by the Son of God in the very act of creation itself. And, as such, it was designed to provide the disciples with the most compelling grounds for fearless faith they could ever have or need.

In Genesis 1:6–10, we see how the triune God brought order to the earth he had newly created. The surging waters were gathered into seas from which the land appeared – the land which was then prepared to be a safe and ideal home for humankind. From the beginning, then, the sea was seen as a hostile, dangerous and unpredictable environment. Throughout the Bible, the image is frequently employed as a metaphor for the forces of evil that range themselves against God and seem poised to reimpose the chaos. This is particularly evident in the book of Psalms, where it is clear that God alone can still the storms of life as they threaten to engulf us:

You answer us with awesome and righteous deeds, God our Saviour, the hope of all the ends of the earth and of the farthest seas, who formed the mountains by your power, having armed yourself with strength, who stilled the roaring of the seas, the roaring of their waves, and the turmoil of the nations (Ps. 65:5–7).

Who is like you, Lord God Almighty? You, Lord, are mighty, and your faithfulness surrounds you. You rule over the surging sea; when its waves mount up, you still them (Ps. 89:8–9).

He stilled the storm to a whisper; the waves of the sea were hushed. They were glad when it grew calm, and he guided them to their desired haven (Ps. 107:29–30).

Most significant of all, thinking in terms of what occurred on the Sea of Galilee, are the dramatic words of Psalm 46, as they describe what seems to be a veritable tsunami:

> God is our refuge and strength, an ever-present help in trouble. Therefore we will not fear, though the earth give way and the mountains fall into the heart of the sea, though its waters roar and foam and the mountains quake with their surging (vv. 1–3).

Again, the chaos of the waters represents the seeming chaos of the world: 'Nations are in uproar, kingdoms fall'. But then comes the massive reassurance: 'he lifts his voice, the earth melts' (v. 6). And what does he say? He says exactly what Jesus said to the winds and the waves in our miracle. 'He says, "Be still, and know that I am God; I will be exalted among the nations, I will be exalted in the earth"' (v. 10).

Oh, I know Jesus simply says, 'Be still!' in Mark 4:39, but it is scarcely credible that those Jewish fishermen, versed as they were from infancy in the Hebrew Scriptures, could have missed the significance of the moment. However, *we* most definitely can! The commonly quoted text 'Be still, and know that I am God' (Ps. 46:10) is also one of the most commonly misinterpreted. These are not primarily words of comfort for the believer. They are not even spoken to believers. They are addressed, just as were Jesus' words on the Sea of Galilee, to the untamed forces of nature which represent those potentially calamitous events and circumstances of life which all of us must face. Reflect on that the next time you see these words on a fridge magnet! Nothing in all God's creation can disturb his peace, or need disturb the peace of his people. As King Canute humbly demonstrated to his fawning courtiers, it is only God who can say to the sea, 'Thus far and no further', safe in the knowledge that there is no power in the universe that can overrule him. It is no wonder we read that, 'The men were amazed and asked, "What kind of man is this? Even the winds and the waves obey him!"' (v. 27). You can almost hear their thought processes! However long it took them, the conclusion was inevitable. Their leader was not simply a man, he was also God!

It is a great blessing to be told in the symbolic language of Revelation 21:1 that in the new heaven and earth there will be 'no longer any sea'. This information is not given in order to ruin any long-term holiday plans you might be making, but to reassure believers that in the eternal state, the risk of any reversal of God's orderly rule will have finally been eliminated. Peace and harmony, *shalom* itself, will reign forever in the new creation.

But, in the meantime, how can we face the very different present reality without fear? There is only one way. Let the staggering truth of who Jesus is begin to fill your mind and soul. If he is in total control of the universe, how can anything you face prove beyond him? If your loving Lord and Saviour is Almighty God, what possible reason can you have to be afraid? Why should your faith not be invincible?

What now?

8

I am sure that the events of that evening were etched deep in the disciples' memories. They would have turned over every element of the story many times in their minds. They would have marvelled, as we have done, at how everything that Jesus did was calculated to dispel their fear and strengthen their faith. And they would have smiled and shaken their heads as they recalled their own spiritual dullness. How much they had needlessly suffered because they had not known Jesus well enough at the time – they had not known him well enough to trust him implicitly, even in the face of the greatest danger.

We must remember that fearless faith is not something we can produce ourselves, any more than we can overcome our troubles and trials by some supreme effort of our will. It is achieved by Christ's work in us. That is why we must always look to him. The key is constantly to grow in our knowledge and love of Jesus.

The Apostle Paul put it succinctly in one famous verse: 'I have been crucified with Christ and I no longer live, but Christ lives in me. The life I now live in the body, I live by faith in the Son of God, who loved me and gave himself for me' (Gal. 2:20). The Christian life can only be lived by faith in Jesus. You may stumble along as best you can with a little faith mixed with fear. Or you may long for something better – a strong and fearless faith that God may choose to use in remarkable ways to serve this generation. Which would you prefer?

But, at the risk of anticlimax, I want to close with a word of encouragement for those whose faith is very weak or virtually non-existent. In the account we've been considering, Jesus may have been frustrated with his disciples' lack of faith. He may even have rebuked them for it. But he did not condemn them. Absolutely anyone reading this little book may echo the disciples' prayer in the boat: 'Lord, save us!' (Mt. 8:25). And Christ will still answer! Even though a violent storm could not wake Jesus, the cries of the desperate always will. It is simply not our Father's intention that any of his little ones should perish.

Union for everyone, for life

If you like what you've read here, check out our website and app. www.uniontheology.org is filled with free, quality resources to bless you.

Our vision is to see the evangelisation of Europe through the raising up of church leaders. To achieve this, our mission under God is to educate and equip pastors, missionaries, church-planters and church-leaders across the continent.

Union offers an affordable, flexible, accessible option for formal theological education.

To find out more, visit:
www.uniontheology.org/courses

 www uniontheology.org

@uniontheology

10Publishing is the publishing house of **10ofThose**.

It is committed to producing quality Christian resources that are biblical and accessible.

www.10ofthose.com is our online retail arm selling thousands of quality books at discounted prices. We also service many church bookstalls and can help your church to set up a bookstall. Single and bulk purchases welcome.

For information contact: **sales@10ofthose.com**

or check out our website: **www.10ofthose.com**